JEREMY CAMP
RESTORED

PIANO · VOCAL · GUITAR

ALAN'S MUSIC CENTER, INC.
8510 La Mesa Blvd.
La Mesa, CA 91941
(619) 466-1938

ISBN 0-634-09521-8

HAL·LEONARD®
CORPORATION
7777 W. BLUEMOUND RD. P.O. BOX 13819 MILWAUKEE, WI 53213

D1292626

Visit Hal Leonard Online at
www.halleonard.com

RESTORED

Words and Music by
JEREMY CAMP

All this time I've wan-dered 'round, search-ing for the things___ I'll nev-er know. I've been

TAKE YOU BACK

Words and Music by
JEREMY CAMP

EVEN WHEN

Words and Music by
JEREMY CAMP

LAY DOWN MY PRIDE

Words and Music by JEREMY CAMP
and JEAN-LUC LAJOIE

Moderately fast

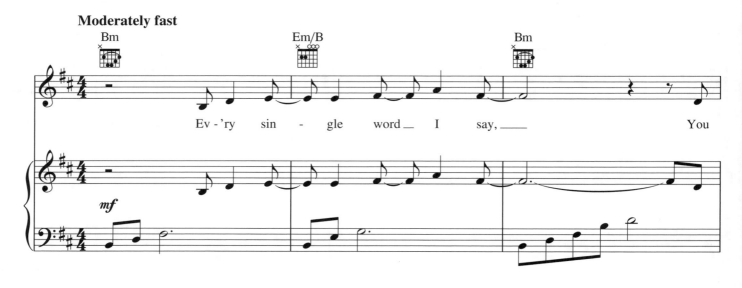

Ev-'ry sin-gle word __ I say, ____ You

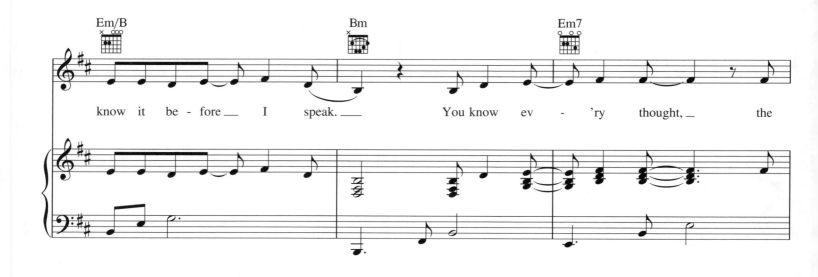

know it be-fore __ I speak. __ You know ev-'ry thought, __ the

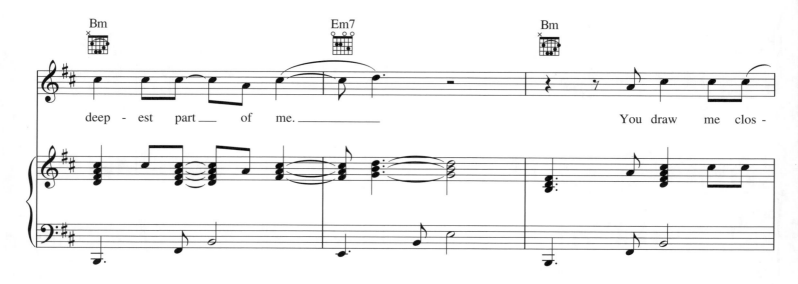

deep-est part __ of me. ____ You draw me clos-

MY DESIRE

Words and Music by
JEREMY CAMP

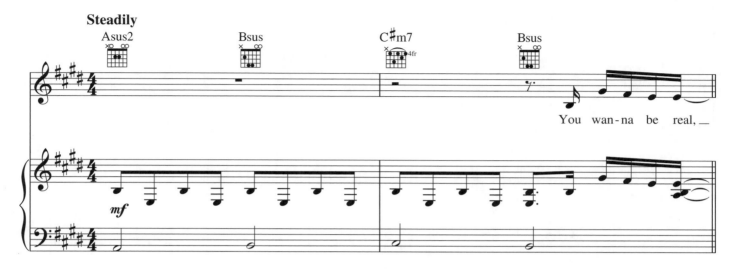

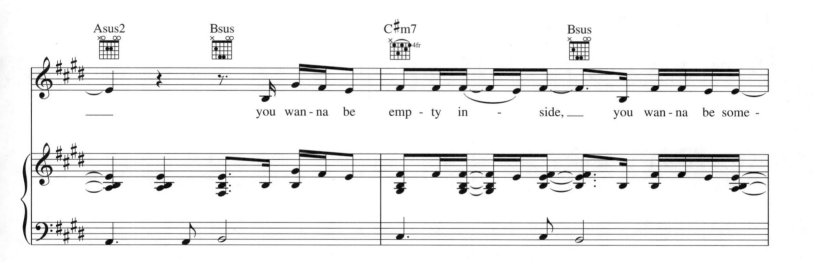

BE THE ONE

Words and Music by
JEREMY CAMP

And all these ___ dreams ___ I've ___ made, ___ I
I know that ___ I ___ have ___ plans, ___ but

take them all ___ and lay them down, in light of rea - sons I ___ have found ___ now.
You will take ___ me ev - 'ry step, for You have cov - ered all ___ my debt ___ now.

I have found ___ that it's ___ the on - ly way. ___

Well, there's more ___ than what ___ I'm feel -

- ing. Well, there's more ___ than what ___ I'm feel -

EVERYTIME

Words and Music by
JEREMY CAMP

to catch a glimpse of this mo - ment.

I hear the sound of this sim - ple plea,

to wait at the feet of Your love.

Ev - 'ry time I'm on my knees,

find You ___ there, ___   find You ___ there. ___

I will find You. _____   I will

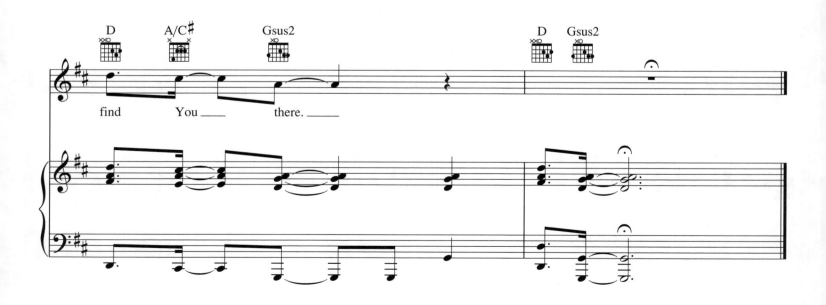

find You ___ there. _____

LETTING GO

Words and Music by
JEREMY CAMP

BREATHE

Words and Music by JEREMY CAMP
and ADAM WATTS

Driving Rock beat

You fill my emp-ty soul, __
You took on ev-'ry-thing __

I'll give You all __ con-trol. __
to make me feel __ com-plete. __

You take this heart of mine __ and
You an-swered ev-'ry call, __ You're

make the piec-es whole. _____
nev-er far __ from reach. _____

You broke this fear in-side, __
You lift me when I fall, __

THIS MAN

Words and Music by
JEREMY CAMP

INNOCENCE

Words and Music by
JEREMY CAMP

Yeah,　　yeah.

NOTHING ELSE I NEED

Words and Music by
JEREMY CAMP